Heroes, Rebels, and Survivors

Mostly True Tales about Growing Up

Larry Castagnola

Illustrated by Bob and Sue Gendron

Resource Publications, Inc.
San Jose, California

Editorial director: Nick Wagner
Editor: Kenneth Guentert
Prepress manager: Elizabeth J. Asborno

Reprint Department
Resource Publications, Inc.
160 E. Virginia Street #290
San Jose, CA 95112-5876

Library of Congress Cataloging in Publication Data
Castagnola, Larry.
    Heroes, rebels, and survivors : mostly true tales about Growing Up / Lawrence Castagnola ; illustrated by Bob and Sue Gendron.
       p.   cm.
    Summary: A collection of twenty-one stories reflecting the author's values of peace, forgiveness, nonviolence, and reconciliation and dealing with a number of moral, political, and social issues.
    ISBN 0-89390-365-5 (pbk.)
    1. Children's stories, American. [1. Conduct of life—Fiction. 2. Short stories.] I. Gendron, Bob, ill. II. Gendron, Sue, ill. III. Title.
PZ7.C26858Co   1996
[Fic]—dc20   95-51520

Printed in the United States of America

00 99 98 97 96 | 5 4 3 2 1

To my nephew, Mike Gendron,
teacher and storyteller,
who was taken from this life by cancer
at the age of thirty-three.

Contents

Preface

When I was a boy, my parents always spoke of the time just before I was born. Historians named those years "The Great Depression." Millions of Americans had no jobs or money. There was a lot of hardship. My parents also talked of their childhood days in the early 1900s, which were also times of hardship. "Children," they reminded me, "carried their shoes to school to save the soles."

This generation of young people is no stranger to hard times, though their feet may be more tender than those of yesteryear. I haven't seen any young people walking barefooted to school to save their shoes. The difficulty for today's young does not lie in material poverty. They have plenty of "stuff." But something vital is missing. Some call that missing thing "values." Others call it "hope."

Surveys taken among children in the lower grades show a fear of dying before reaching teenage years. The increased number of young people who die from random violence has created another kind of "great depression." We live in a society in which a person's life is sometimes held less valuable than a pair of expensive basketball shoes or a jacket with the logo of a professional team. In a very real sense, this generation of young people "has it worse" than their parents or my parents.

In this collection of stories, I explore some of the events of my own adolescence as well as the experiences of young people I have known over the years. All of these stories, including the one about the goose, are based on true life experiences. My intention in presenting them is to help young readers reflect on their own lives with humor and hope for the future. My stories ask the reader to consider values of nonviolence, peace, forgiveness, and reconciliation. Hopefully, the student will reflect on the kind of world he or she wants to live in and realize these values can be achieved and bring great personal happiness along with a better world.

The Chase

The year was 1972. I had been smooth-faced all my life but at the age of forty I grew a beard. It was a time when beards were not that popular in the United States except among members of certain religious groups, professors, back-to-nature types such as "hippies" and those who found shaving a nuisance. In my home town of Sacramento, some people identified beards with people who used illegal drugs. It was a time when teenagers who wanted to let their hair grow long were suspended from schools and often thrown out of their family homes.

In the year of 1972 my "bearded self" was waiting outside a record store for two of the teenagers who lived in my group home. I was standing by my car when approached by two men who appeared to be in their early thirties. They both were rather glassy-eyed and their speech was not too coherent as they asked me: "Know where we can get some grass?"

"Grass?" Were they doing some landscaping? No. It was clear they wanted marijuana. Instead of just answering, "I don't know," I decided to become sarcastic, a wiseguy. Here I was, a religious role model running a group home for teenagers with drug problems, and these men perceived me to be a drug dealer or someone "with connections."

"There's a guy," I said, "named Duane Lowe. He picks up a lot of marijuana. You might try him. He might give you some."

Duane Lowe was the local sheriff.

One of the two realized I was being a wiseguy. I was in deep trouble. First one and then both started to come after me with rage in their eyes. I got in my car and pulled out as they were banging on my doors.

As I sped out of the parking lot they followed me in hot pursuit. I was speeding in traffic but the two were right on my tail in their Ford Falcon. I wished for a policeman to stop me so I could escape my pursuers. No luck. I was on my own. In and out of traffic we went. Recalling some chase scenes from movies, I made a radical U-turn and went in the opposite direction. The determined drug addicts in their Ford Falcon could not keep up with me. For the moment I had outwitted them.

I drove back to the record store where I had left the two boys from my group home. They were standing outside when I pulled up with the command: "Get in, quick. Two guys are after me."

The boys found my situation humorous. For once I was the one in crisis.

"You see how your beard got you in trouble. You need a shave."

The boy who made that comment was Bruce. With his blond hair flowing shoulder length, he had been turned in to the juvenile authorities by his parents as being "beyond control" because he refused to have his hair cut. When I first started the home, I had threatened the boys with haircuts if they got involved with drugs. On one occasion I followed through with my threat and gave haircuts to six boys who were caught using drugs. But now it was my turn to part with my prized beard.

Not long after the chase, I did remove my beard. I made the event a kind of ceremony, allowing my nieces and nephews to participate in the shave.

Not too many years later, beards were once again fashionable among teachers and preachers and all the other "straight" people. Even once conservative schools allowed male students to wear their hair long. But in 1972 too much hair on your face or head was a sign you belonged to the Evil Drug Empire. My beard, coupled with a smart remark, almost cost me my life. Such is the changing nature of the world we live in. When it became okay to wear long hair and grow beards, many of the young men began to shave their heads. The bald look became the "in thing." "Bald is beautiful" became the slogan of basketball players and college professors, just in time for those of us losing our hair.

As for the two guys in the Ford Falcon, I never did see them again. If either or both of them happen to read this story, my message is: "No hard feelings."

Questions for Discussion

1. Have you known someone with a drug problem? Describe the situation.

2. Have you ever made a sarcastic remark that got you into trouble or caused trouble for someone else? Describe the situation.

3. Do you think one's hair style or form of grooming prejudices you one way or another about what you expect from that person?

4. Have you ever had to run from someone who threatened you? Describe the situation.

Harry the Hamster

Harry the Hamster was born in captivity. That's how he came to be known as "Harry," for hamsters in the wild have names such as "Slurp," "Giggles," or "Mophead." Harry's humanized habitat was the bedroom of a girl named D. Lynne.

Harry, to my knowledge, did not have any traumatic experiences in the girl's bedroom. Perched in a cage on her dresser, he had a rodent palace. Yet he was still in a wilderness, since D. Lynne was not a punctilious room cleaner. (Few thirteen-year-old girls are. Her mother said the bedroom contained "dinosaur dust.") Despite it all, Harry appeared happy and secure in his cage, even though the girl's room was primeval chaos.

D. Lynne had a TV in her room and she often watched *National Geographic.* So Harry grew up watching programs about baby skunks, baby porcupines, baby giraffes, and even baby lions. He saw how little animals in the wild learned to play and find food. He was amazed by how much play there was between the brothers and sisters of the animal world. While D. Lynne allowed him on her lap during TV time, most of the day and night Harry was confined to his cage. He had food and water, a trapeze, and a plastic tube tunnel. Every human effort was made to create for him a "hamster haven."

Harry appeared content, but deep in his soul there was a dark problem.

D. Lynne did her best to love Harry. It was difficult for her to turn him over to a "hamster sitter" when she went on vacation with her family. She got her uncle to take care of him for the few weeks that she was away. His instructions were simply to feed him. He was not expected to watch TV with the hamster or take it for a walk. Unfortunately, her uncle forgot to close Harry's cage properly after one of his meals. Harry escaped.

The first thing D. Lynne did on returning home was to call her uncle to find out what happened to Harry. Her uncle was embarrassed as he rushed over to help search for the runaway.

"Get me three thirty-gallon garbage bags," barked the uncle upon entering the bedroom.

"What for?" asked D. Lynne.

"One is for your dirty laundry, one for your games and things, and the third for trash." The uncle had volunteered for hurricane cleanup in Florida and believed he could handle the situation.

Uncle and niece worked for two full hours, clearly expecting to find Harry hiding under a towel or in a shoe. After the cleaning was done and all obstacles had been removed from the room, there was still no sign of Harry. Uncle and niece were convinced that the worst had happened, that he had left the house and become a meal for a stray cat. (The family cat was not suspect because he ate only expensive canned cat foods.)

As they walked out of the room carrying the garbage bags, an amazing thing happened. Harry, who as it turns out was hiding in the shower, walked into his bedroom and went straight up into his cage.

"He was just waiting for us to leave. He waited until his room was cleaned," commented the uncle.

"Are you hinting I should take better care of my room?" said D. Lynne.

The uncle had a habit of not answering certain kinds of questions and he said nothing. But from that day onward D. Lynne kept her room so clean that her mother invited members of the local women's environmental club to hold their monthly meetings in the company of Harry.

At one of the meetings, the president of the environmental club said: "I believe that Harry, despite having lived in a human's subhuman den, has thrived as a rodent. It was only when the humanoid room became so chaotic that his instinct directed him to find another habitat."

D. Lynne listened to the woman's words and added: "You mean hamsters choke and gag at the sight and smell of a dirty room?"

"I didn't want to put it so bluntly, my dear, but I think you finally have understood what happens when an animal habitat is downgraded to the level of 'teenager's room'."

Questions for Discussion

1. What are the rules, if any, for the room you live in? How are they enforced?

2. If you had your choice between these two saying to hand on your wall, which would you choose and why?

   • Cleanliness is next to godliness.
   • A clean room is the sign of a sick mind.

3. Do you think animals have rights? Give an example to back up your answer.

4. What happens to humans when their natural habitat is taken away? Give an example from U.S. history.

The Boy from El Salvador

W hen Pedro walked into Matthew's home in Sacramento, California, in 1988, it was the first time he had ever been in a house with electricity and running water. Pedro's house had no light, not even windows. It had dirt floors and was shared with the family chickens, ducks, and pigs. Pedro was from the countryside of El Salvador. He was fourteen years old, but because of poor nutrition he was small for his age and looked much younger. He was brought to the United States by an organization that gave medical help to victims of war. Pedro had pieces of metal in his arms and chest from the explosion of a land mine in his village. He had stepped on the explosive while gathering firewood. Like thousands of other children throughout the world where there has been war, Pedro had fragments of metal from the mine in his body. While he was not in danger of death, he could not lead a normal life of work and play.

During the days that Pedro stayed with Matthew, he drew pictures of his village and his home. Matthew also liked to draw. Pedro was amazed at how Matthew could draw pictures of fancy automobiles from the 1950s with great detail. The two boys did not speak the same language, but they communicated through pictures and photos. Since Pedro did not have photos of his village, he drew all his pictures for Matthew from memory. Most of the time Pedro drew sketches of farm animals, trees, and simple houses made of sticks and palm branch roofs.

One day Pedro and Matthew were sitting in Doctor D.'s office. It was Doctor D. who had donated his services and made the operation possible. While waiting for the doctor, Pedro began to draw a helicopter. Matthew watched him while he sketched. He was not copying it from another picture. After drawing the broad outline of the plane, Pedro began to fill in the details, which included a machine gun. Matthew was rather surprised by Pedro's drawing, which had a lot of detail, more detail than his sketch of a 1954 Cadillac. How, he wondered, could a boy from a land that did not even have running water draw such a perfect picture of a machine that was made in the United States of America? Pedro lived in a poor village and had never seen a flushing toilet or an electric stove. How was it that he could sketch sophisticated weapons?

When Pedro finished his drawing, it turned out to be not a very happy one. Below the helicopter were people running in every direction. The sky was filled with dots like black snow flakes. Matthew wondered why Pedro was drawing such a sad scene. Matthew had no experience of war, except what he saw on TV. Pedro had never watched TV or read a daily paper. But he knew all the details of a warplane.

After Doctor D. attended to all of Pedro's medical needs, the boy had to return to his village. Parting from Matthew was difficult. It was Matthew who showed him how to shoot a basketball and throw an American football. It was Matthew who introduced him to pizza and jazz, roller-skating and billiards. The two boys shook hands at the airport, sensing that they would never see each other again.

When Pedro returned to his village, he was homesick for Matthew and his friends in the United States. In his village no one paid too much attention

to him. His elders commented: "Now that you have the metal taken from your body by your rich friends in the United States, you can go into the fields and work."

Pedro continued to draw pictures and send them to Matthew. The boys were able to share their life experiences because Matthew had the opportunity to learn Spanish at school. Matthew went to college and took a special interest in the history of Pedro's country. He discovered among other things that the machine gun sketched by Pedro was also built in the United States of America by the same company that made his family's stove, refrigerator, and light bulbs.

Matthew wrote to the President of the United States and asked that weapons not be sent to El Salvador. After a while the United States did stop sending weapons, thanks to government officials who listened to Matthew and other people who loved Pedro's country.

Peace finally came in 1992 to El Salvador. Many people from the United States of America and other countries of the world went there to find, remove, and destroy all the hidden land mines that might still explode and injure more children like Pedro.

Pedro still writes to Matthew after many years. He talks about the improvements being made in his village. He still draws pictures, but children dancing under electric lights have replaced the grim drawings of gunships.

Questions for Discussion

1. Have you ever known anyone who grew up or spent time in a foreign country? What did you learn about a different culture?

2. Imagine moving to a place without electrical service. List some ways your life would be different from the way it is now.

3. If you were asked to sketch a moment of your life that was very fearful, what would you draw?

4. Why would Pedro be justified in his fear of going to school in the countryside in El Salvador? Do we have things we might call "land mines" in some of our cities?

How the Tooth Fairy
Almost Lost Her Job

Red and Syd were twin brothers who looked so
much alike their mother had to put name tags
on their shirts so she could call them by their names
instead of saying: "Hey, you." It was only when they
became old men that they were easy to tell apart. Red
still had his hair at the age of eighty, while Syd was
as bald as a worn-out basketball. As old men, they
told their grandchildren stories about their lives. One
of their favorites was called: "How the Tooth Fairy
Almost Lost Her Job." It went like this:

"We were children in the days of radio before TV
was born," said the old men to their grandchildren.
"In those days there was a Saturday program called
Uncle Wobill. We listened to the program especially
on our birthdays or when we lost our baby teeth
because Uncle Wobill would tell us where to find
presents. He was an amazing man, that Wobill. He
could tell children to look in their closets or under
their beds and, sure enough, the present would be
there just as he directed."

There were toothless smiles on the faces of the old
twins as they continued their story.

"It happened one day when we were listening to
the program that Uncle Wobill told us to put our baby
teeth under our pillows at night. If we had been good,

the Tooth Fairy would take the teeth and leave a present under our pillows. We were five years old at the time and had our baby teeth in a jar because our mom had told us to save them. We did as Uncle Wobill said. We put our teeth beneath our pillows and fell asleep believing in Uncle Wobill. We didn't know if the fairy was a man or a woman, but we guessed a woman. We wondered what she wanted with little kids' teeth. We guessed she made necklaces or bracelets with them. What else would a fairy do with so many teeth? Or maybe she recycled them and gave them to dogs and cats who had no teeth.

"The next morning we found our presents beneath our pillows. We each got a shiny silver cap gun with a supply of caps. There was a note which said:

> Good Morning, My Little Cowboys.
> Your Friend, T. F.

"We thought the note was a little strange. We didn't know the Tooth Fairy was our friend. But we liked the guns. We had always played Cops and Robbers or Cowboys and Indians using our thumbs and index fingers as guns and yelling, 'Bang, bang, you're dead.' Now with our shiny new silver guns we yelled all the louder: 'Bang, bang, you're dead.' We were pretty weird little kids. But those were the days before television. We loved our games.

"In those days there was no preschool, so we waited until we were six years old before entering kindergarten. Every day was play day for us. We had a big yard and lots of trees to climb, so we did a lot of running around shooting our guns and making up new games, always with good guys capturing the bad guys. We didn't understand that in real life sometimes the bad guys got away.

"It happened that in our neighborhood there were some real bad guys who were robbing neighborhood homes. Our parents got scared and bought a real gun to protect our home. We didn't know our parents had a real gun. They kept it locked up, except at night when they had it ready to use against any real robbers. They didn't want us kids to know where the gun was hidden.

"Then one night our parents were invited to their high school class reunion. They didn't go out much. But when they did, they called in Deirdre, the babysitter, to watch us. My parents told Deirdre about the robberies in the neighborhood. But they did not tell her about the real gun they kept in the house. They told her to call the police if there was any problem.

"At eight p.m. Deirdre sent us off to bed. Our bedroom was upstairs next to our parents' room. She stayed downstairs doing her homework. Both of us tried to go to sleep, but we could not. Deirdre was listening to some music while she was doing her homework and it kept us awake. We went into our parents' bedroom to play on their bed. They had a big bed and it was fun to jump on it. So that's what we did. Then, lo and behold, we found a gun that looked exactly like the ones the Tooth Fairy had given us. It seemed heavier than ours. It was under Dad's pillow. For us, all guns were play guns. We agreed to scare our babysitter with our parents' gun.

"We took our parents' gun along with our own guns and crept slowly down the stairs. Deirdre was sitting at a desk with her back to us. When we got to the bottom of the stairs we yelled: 'Bang, bang, you're dead.' We shot our cap guns and our parents' gun. Luck was on our side because the cap gun went off first and Deirdre hit the floor seconds before a real bullet tore through the back of the chair she was sitting in. She screamed at us to drop our guns. We knew she was serious. We dropped our guns and ran to her. She then called the police and our parents.

17

"The police got to our house before our parents. They asked us a lot of questions about the real gun. We really did not know the answers. We thought the Tooth Fairy gave our parents a bad gun. We thought all guns came from the Tooth Fairy. What did we know? The police asked us about Uncle Wobill and our toy guns. I remember an officer saying: 'These cap guns look like the real McCoy.' We didn't know anyone named McCoy. We guessed he was a friend of Uncle Wobill or the Tooth Fairy. We were really confused.

"Our parents finally came home. They were very embarrassed to see the police. Our mother sort of confessed that she gave the Tooth Fairy wrong information about us wanting cap guns. She said the Tooth Fairy made a mistake and was supposed to give us gum instead of guns. We didn't understand how our parents communicated with the Tooth Fairy. Mother said that whether you're dealing with Santa Claus or the Tooth Fairy, it is best to put things in writing and have a spell-check done on your list.

"Our dad apologized to us, our babysitter, and to the police for leaving a loaded gun under his pillow. Then the police asked him a rather strange question: 'Can you right now tell the difference between your twins?' Our dad had to admit he could not. He looked to our mother for help. 'Then how,' the police continued, 'did you expect your boys to tell the difference between their toy guns and your real one? They look exactly alike in the dark. Twins are twins, even when it comes to guns.'

"Our father was really sorry for what he had done. He gave his gun to the police and he told them to tell his story to other children. He wrote a personal letter to Uncle Wobill apologizing to the Tooth Fairy for harming her reputation. When we woke up the next morning we looked under our pillows and there was a

note from the Tooth Fairy with a bag of bubble gum.
The note read:

> Both of you are better boys
> for turning in your bang-bang toys.
> Blow a bugle, beat a drum.
> Pop a bubble with your gum.
> Beware of bullets that are real
> for they your precious life will steal.

"So, grandchildren, that is a true story of what happened to us when we were kids. It had a happy ending. No one was hurt. We all learned a lesson. And the Tooth Fairy kept in touch with us, always writing us nice notes and giving us gum for our good behavior. And she keeps up this practice even today. We were happy she did not lose her job. By the way, kids, care for some gum?"

Questions for Discussion

1. Have you ever been in a situation involving a gun which turned out to be more dangerous than you imagined? Explain.

2. Have you ever injured anyone accidentally?

3. What are the responsibilities of parents who have guns in their homes?

4. Do you think toy guns are appropriate gifts for children? Explain your opinion.

The Beautiful Vulture

In the countryside of Central America lived a citizen of Scotland who had been there as a teacher for many years. His students were boys and girls who worked most of their days on large coffee plantations. These boys and girls had little time for study because they worked sixteen-hour days for pennies.

The teacher would go from village to village on his motorcycle and teach his tired students in the evenings. The Scot taught them the history of his own country, how his Scottish and Irish ancestors had struggled against unjust landlords. He told them how many of his island countrymen crossed the Atlantic Ocean to find a new life in the Americas. He told them of the conquistadores who plundered for gold, silver, and other things that would make them rich. The teacher knew much about history and the struggles of native peoples to regain their freedom. He would always end his lessons by saying: "We must pray and work that everyone may be free."

Not everyone in Central America loved the teacher from Scotland. Many who owned large plantations heard his stories of freedom and were worried that the students would want the freedom he taught. They did not want to pay a minimum wage or grant paid vacations. They wanted their workers to continue to work for pennies. They loved profits more than their

workers. They hated the teacher enough to kill him. The only reason they did not kill him was their fear that the government of Scotland might lead a boycott of their coffee.

So the wealthy plantation owners hatched a plot. They said: "This Scotsman turns the students against us. He puts into their minds ideas of freedom and justice for the peasants. The young people are restless because of him. They will want shorter work days and more pay. We must eliminate this meddling foreigner from our midst. But we must not anger his fellow countrymen. We must make his death look like an accident. We will hire a soldier to shoot him on a lonely road as he rides his motorcycle from village to village. Then we will say that a hunter accidentally shot him while chasing a wild pig."

Some students heard of the plot and told the teacher that his life was in danger. They told him that he should be very careful when he was in the areas controlled by soldiers. While the teacher was frightened, he did not stop teaching.

One day he was traveling alone on his motorcycle along a dusty trail. He was wearing his helmet and was on the lookout for soldiers. He knew where the military had its checkpoints. He did everything he could think of to be safe. He came to a turn in the road and saw ahead of him a huge vulture eating the remains of some small animal. Now the Scotsman liked most animals. He did not particularly like bats because they would keep him awake at night, flying in his room and buzzing over him. He did not like the snakes he saw on the trails, but he always felt safe because he wore thick motorcycle boots. He did not like vultures. But this dislike, he admitted, was due to their looks and their diet. The vulture who circled overhead looking for the flesh of dead animals to eat was not the kind of bird he would choose for a pet.

The teacher slowed down as he approached the vulture on the road. But just as he was a few feet away the vulture flew straight into his helmet and knocked him off his motorcycle. At that instant a shot rang out from a wooded area on the hill ahead of him. The teacher and the vulture both lay dazed on the road as bullets flew overhead. Realizing that the bullets were meant for him and not the vulture, the teacher quickly got back on his motorcycle and headed back in the direction away from the bullets. He counted twenty shots aimed at himself. He drove his motorcycle in a zigzag manner to avoid being hit. He made it to one of the villages. He was not hurt except for a few bruises.

That evening when he was surrounded by his students in a village, he told them the story of the vulture. He had passed by many vultures in his lifetime. He confessed that he had always thought of them as ugly. But now he thought of them as beautiful—"pretty as peacocks" was the expression he actually used. He called his experience "How a Vulture Became a Guardian Angel." He told his students they had to fear nothing from bats, snakes, and vultures but only from the people who were poor imitations of the creatures of the wild.

The teacher eventually left Central America and went back to his native land to raise money for his poor students on the coffee plantations. Whenever he spoke to a group about the needs of his students, he always kept a vulture feather in his hand, handling it as if it were a pencil or a cigarette. Someone would always ask him: "Why do you carry a feather?" Then he would tell them his story of the Beautiful Vulture and how his life was saved on a dusty trail in the middle of nowhere when bullets came flying.

Questions for Discussion

1. How might this story have ended if the students had not liked and cared for their teacher?

2. Does this story illustrate the saying, "Beauty is in the eye of the beholder"? Explain.

3. Would you refer to a cold-blooded murderer as an "animal"? Explain why you would or would not use that word.

4. Describe someone who stands out in your memory as a good teacher.

The Winemaker

Once there was a man who planted a vineyard. After several years of hard work, the man was successful in producing beautiful vines. The wines from his vineyard were acclaimed throughout the world. The man had a talent for developing his vineyard. He personally planted his vines and made sure the soil was just right for producing grapes that were sweet and abundant.

The winemaker poured all his personal and family resources into making his business a success. He treated his workers fairly, paying them a just wage with medical benefits. He used no dangerous pesticides and stayed true to his ideal of producing good wines.

It happened one day that a young man drove his car off the road and crashed into the winemaker's vineyard and winery, causing several thousand dollars' worth of damage. The young man, it was said, was a high school dropout and was drunk at the time of the accident. Fortunately, he was wearing his seat belt and survived without a scratch.

The community's reaction to the property damage was immediate. One of the winemaker's friends said: "It is time to make laws that would punish high school dropouts. The whipping post worked in the past. We need to bring back the good old days." Many people agreed with this kind of thinking.

Another said: "We need to build more prisons. That no-good dropout should be put away so he will not be in a position to harm anyone in the future."

A third friend commented: "In some countries they beat such youth with canes. We should do the same."

The winemaker listened to the advice of his friends. But after careful consideration, he rejected their way of thinking. Instead, he presented a letter to the juvenile judge.

"Honorable judge of the juvenile court," he wrote, "I have decided not to press charges against the young man who caused fifty thousand dollars' worth of damage to my vineyard and winery. Instead, I ask the court to allow me to make a deal with the young man. I will pay his way through college. If he completes college and has his bachelor's degree in five years, he owes no restitution and his education remains a gift."

The judge liked the idea, but the winemaker's friends thought he had lost his mind. To his friends, the winemaker said: "I know you think that physical punishment and jail time is the way to right the wrongs we suffer. But to my way of thinking, a teenager is like a young vine. If you give it the right soil, fertilize it, and prune it properly, you get beautiful grapes. If you leave it to fight for its life on bad soil with no water, it will die or produce inferior grapes. Shouldn't I show as much concern for this young man as I do for my vines?"

The man's friends were stunned by his words and had nothing further to say.

The winemaker continued: "Sure, I am taking a risk by giving a college education to a high school dropout. But if each of us does not take risks for the future of the great vineyard—I'm talking about our planet—we will have no sweet grapes and new wines but only inferior raisins and vinegar."

As an extra bonus, the Winemaker gave the dropout a summer job in the vineyard so he could make enough money to get his car repaired. As expected, the Winemaker insisted that any future drinking and driving would mean "no deal" for the college scholarship and charges would be pressed for the damages to his vineyard and winery.

The dropout surprised even himself by finishing college in four years. He took an interest in chemistry and got over his need to experiment on himself with drugs. The Winemaker was so impressed that he hired the young man as an assistant to his chemist. He even named one of his new varietal wines "The Graduate." On the label of the new wine he added to the government-required warning about pregnancy, possible birth defects, and impaired judgment this quotation from the former dropout: "I almost made my life a mess by drinking to excess."

Questions for Discussion

1. Were you ever given another change when you thought you had struck out in some situation? Describe the situation.

2. Have you ever been tempted to drop out of school? What keeps you motivated to try in school?

3. Was the Winemaker a socially responsible person? Was he soft on crime? Explain your opinions.

4. Comment on the proper use and the misuse of alcohol.

How the Weeping Willow Got Its Name

A very special tree is found in many places of the world; it is named the "weeping willow." It is a very beautiful tree with long thin branches that bend over, giving the tree the appearance of being an umbrella. Not only does the tree grow very quickly, but it is generous in reproducing itself. All you have to do is break off a branch, put it in water for a while, and then plant it. The branches root so easily that anyone can successfully plant a weeping willow.

The weeping willow makes many people happy with its generous shade. How then did it come to be called the "weeping" willow and not the "happy" or "umbrella" willow? No one knows for sure why the name "weeping" was given to it. A man once gave me this explanation. He assured me it was a true story.

"Once I had one of those willow trees in the back yard of my family home. I had four daughters who loved to play with their friends in our yard near the tree. The children played the same games of most children: hide-and-seek and so forth. They also liked to jump rope. One day when my girls couldn't find their jump rope, they broke a few branches off the willow tree and used them for ropes. I recognized that branch breaking could lead to abuses and warned them not to break off any more branches. The girls promised to obey.

"The willow tree seemed happy that I was now its self-appointed protector. Then a few of the boys in the neighborhood got the idea that it would be fun to play a game they called 'Zorro.' They had just seen a movie about a man who wore a black cape, black hat, and black shoes and who had only one weapon, a whip. Like many children, they wanted to imitate their movie hero. They admired Zorro for being able to disarm gunmen with the swift snap of his whip. The branches of the willow tree made perfect whips. The boys broke off so many branches that my willow tree was almost reduced to a stump. I was very angry. I apologized to the willow and warned my daughters that their friends could no longer play in the yard.

"'If either you girls or the boys who play in this yard tear off one more branch, I am going to cut down the tree. I will not allow a mutilated and unhappy tree in our back yard.'

"I did not want to cut down the tree. I knew my daughters loved the tree, especially my third girl, Jackson.

"'Daddy, please don't cut down our tree. I love the willow.' There were tears in Jackson's eyes as she pleaded for mercy and understanding. She promised to stop the 'Zorromania.'

"As the days passed, the boys did not quit their game. They went into my back yard without the girls' permission. They stripped every last branch from the willow. I was angry enough to follow through with my threat to cut down the tree. So one afternoon when all the girls were home I told them that the tree was to be cut down. I took out my chainsaw and began sharpening the chain with a file. I had been filing only a few minutes when I noticed that Jackson left the room. I asked her sisters to go and find her. I was afraid that she was running away from home. My

other daughters went out into the yard and came back with the message: 'Jackson has climbed the tree. She says she will stay in the tree until you promise not to cut it down. She says that she will go down with her tree.'

"I didn't say anything. I kept on sharpening my saw. I had been in the air force. I knew of captains who bravely went down with their planes to save the lives of crewmembers or civilians on the ground. I knew that Jackson loved the willow tree and she could not control the Zorro craze of the neighborhood boys.

"I went out into the yard. I called to Jackson to come down. She refused to come down from the top of the mutilated tree.

"'Jackson, come down. This poor tree has been torn apart. The only thing it's good for is to be cut down. I'm going to cut it down. So get down from the tree.'

"My girl could be stubborn when she believed in something. She believed in her tree. Her lip stiffened as she said: 'If you cut down the tree, you will have to cut it with me in it.' Her silent tears rolling down the trunk of the tree told me how much she cared for her tree.

"I realized I was being too hard in threatening to cut down the tree. I decided to change my tactics. After all, neither Jackson nor the tree was at fault. It was the boys stripping the branches for their Zorro whips who needed the lesson.

"'Ok, Jackson, you can come down. I am not going to cut down the tree. I promise.'

"My daughter came down. I kept my promise. I called the neighborhood boys together. I told them they would each have to plant their own willow trees in their own yards. I told them I did not want to see them again in my yard until their own trees were at least two feet tall. The boys had no choice but to agree.

"This is not where my story ends. In the months to come, Jackson would go to the tree every day and ask forgiveness for what her friends did to it. Sometimes she would cry and moisten the tree with her tears. Her sisters called the willow her 'weeping tree.'

"Many of the townsfolk began calling my willow tree the 'weeping willow' because of Jackson's tears. Because I made the neighborhood boys put their Zorro whips in water to sprout roots, they planted their whips. Every house on our street had at least one willow tree. That's why the elders of our town decided to change the name of our street to 'Weeping Willow Way.'"

That, my friends, is how the ordinary willow tree became known as the "weeping willow." Now some old-timers might have another explanation, but I believe I have given you the correct history.

Questions for Discussion

1. Describe a situation in which you or someone you know stood up for what was right.

2. Why do you think the dad overcame his pride and changed his mind about cutting down the tree?

3. Have you ever been in a situation in which you felt powerless about the behavior of your friends and did not stand up for what was right? Describe the situation.

4. What are some ways people in our society misuse natural resources? What efforts have you made to conserve nature?

Operation Treehouse

Tyrone was Juana's older brother by one year. Though raised in the inner city, they had a treehouse which gave them a kind of other-world experience which Juana described as "living with eagles." As children of professional parents, both of them did well in school. Their father was a colonel in the army; their mother, a teacher. They were permitted their nest as long as their grades were good.

Though they both had excellent school records, Tyrone blew it in the eighth grade. He developed an interest in exploring some abandoned mine shafts along with some storm drains not too far from school. After missing several days of school due to his explorations, his teacher warned him about expulsion. Not only did he not listen, he led other students through the drains and caves during class time. He was expelled.

The expulsion didn't hurt Tyrone because just then his father was transferred to duty in Turkey, so he and Juana entered the army base schools. There were no distractions in the new and foreign environment. Both he and Juana graduated from high school with honors.

Juana and Tyrone went back to the United States. She studied to become a nurse and he joined the army. He wasn't sure if he wanted to follow in his father's footsteps, but he gave the military a try.

After a few years in the army, he was sent to fight in
Vietnam. While he was there, he had an experience
which changed his direction in life. One day he was in
a skirmish in which his platoon killed several
civilians. Then and there he decided to leave the
army. His military superiors told him he couldn't just
leave, but he did anyway. In a sense, it was his eighth
grade all over again. He was expelled. But this time,
he was not endangering his friends by leading them
through dangerous mine shafts. He wanted instead to
be a peacemaker. He expected rejection by his father
and was surprised when he said, "There's more than
one way to be patriotic."

After a few months in the military jail (the "brig")
and a dishonorable discharge, Tyrone went to night
school to pursue studies in military history. He
wanted to find out more about why wars began and
the psychology of violence. In four years he was
teaching a college course in the history of warfare.

In 1980 Juana, who was a practicing nurse in a
community of Indians in Central America, was killed
by security forces. Tyrone was devastated and began
an investigation of her death. He went to the place of
her death and his trail of investigation led him to
conclude that not only his sister's death but the
deaths of many other innocent civilians were the
responsibility of military officers trained in a special
school financed unknowingly by himself as a U.S.
taxpayer.

When he completed his investigation, he gave the
results of his finding to his congressman:

> The "MP" in the name of this school does
> not stand for "Mary Poppins." It's supposed
> to be a military police academy, but in
> reality "MP" means "many problems."
> Evidence I've uncovered shows that
> hundreds of graduates go on to torture and

kill innocent civilians in their home countries. Do we need to sponsor such an officer training school?

Tyrone's congressman answered him in these words:

The school is part of our hemispheric strategy. The army knows what it is doing in training foreign soldiers to fight communism. I will continue to support the MP School.

Tyrone was not discouraged. He knew he had to continue in the struggle in memory of his sister. It was twenty years since he led his fellow eighth graders through the forbidden storm drains. He wondered what nonviolent act he could do to call attention to the MP School. The answer came to him in a dream in which he saw Juana calling him from their tree house. He knew the symbolic meaning of the dream.

That morning he went to "Ranger Joe's," a military supply store. He bought himself an officer's uniform. From there he went to the base where the MP School for foreign soldiers was located. Sporting his newly purchased uniform, he walked on the base. He felt strange when enlisted men saluted him as though he was his father.

It was dusk when Tyrone, with a boombox on his back, climbed a tree over the barracks of sleeping Central American trainees. He waited in the tree for several hours, thinking of Juana and saying, "This one is for you, sister." At four a.m., an hour before the soldiers were to awaken, he turned on his boombox at full volume. In Spanish, the voice came out loud and clear: "Soldiers, stop killing your brothers and sisters. You do not have to obey anyone who orders you to kill your brother."

Within a few minutes, Tyrone was handcuffed and arrested. The judge sentenced him to three years in a federal prison for trespassing and impersonating an officer. He served eighteen months of the three-year sentence. He was never bitter about the prison time. In his heart he knew he had taken the higher moral ground. He could not bring his sister back to life, but he could help to prevent others from dying as she did.

After all Tyrone's effort, the military school was not closed, although more than one hundred members of Congress, inspired by Tyrone's steadfastness, voted to close the school. It was their way of saying to the American people: "We agree with the message Tyrone played that early morning of Operation Treehouse."

Tyrone today still continues his crusade to close the MP School. Each year he persuades a few more members of Congress to agree with his point of view. Whether or not the school is ever closed, he has proven to many Americans that patriotism comes in many forms, involves risks, and may even result in jail time.

Questions for Discussion

1. What are the qualities you admire or do not admire in Tyrone?

2. Do you think a school should be judged by the quality of its graduates? Discuss.

3. Were Tyrone's actions of trespassing and impersonating an officer morally justifiable, in your opinion? Why would you say he was or was not patriotic?

4. What are your personal opinions about conscientious objection to participating in a particular war? Can you identify any people now

considered great Americans who went to jail for
their protest against war or injustice?

The Teardrop Kid

A boy who once lived with me was a seventeen-year-old named Jose, but I called him "the Teardrop Kid." The nickname was easy to pick because Jose had a teardrop tattooed beneath his right eye.

Jose had no other tattoos on his body, just the one teardrop. I really did not know why he had such a tattoo. I did not ask him.

Jose came from a tough, inner-city neighborhood. Like many children from the ghetto, he was forced into participating in a gang. He was only nine when older gang members initiated him. The tattoo, I learned later, meant he pulled the trigger in a gangland shootout in which a young person was killed. I didn't think of Jose as a killer. Yet he may have been involved in a shootout. I suspected that he wanted to appear tough, a real gangster, so he had the tattoo done.

My home for boys was called a "group home." This was a little different from a foster home. In a foster home a boy or girl is expected to relate to a foster parent. Sometimes the boys and girls are expected to call the foster parents "mom" and "dad." This is very difficult for teenagers who have a hard time relating to any adults. For the boys and girls who had a lot of trouble in foster homes, there were group homes. In such a home a young person could get help for his or

40

her problems but not have to worry about relating to a father or mother.

The juvenile probation authorities sent Jose to my home so he could get out of his old neighborhood, get away from his old friends, and, hopefully, finish high school. In my home he had some supervision and was given help to finish high school.

A rule we had in our home was "no alcohol, no drugs." One Friday night the boys pooled their allowances and bought some beer to drink. This kind of thing happens often in group homes. Sometimes young staff members who want to be popular allow the rules to be broken. On this particular Friday evening, I was alone with the boys. It was obvious to me they had been drinking beer. They were caught and, like a traffic cop, I had to give citations.

According to the rules, Jose lost his privilege of visiting his family home. He begged me not to take away his home visit. He pleaded with me, even shed a few real tears, but I did not change his penalty. I did not feel too badly about this punishment because his parents paid no attention to him when he did go on a home visit. He would more than likely get in trouble with his old friends.

About a half hour after Jose pleaded with me in vain, he came knocking on my door. He was holding his arm to stop blood from a cut.

"What happened?" I asked. I saw he had a deep cut on his wrist.

"I did it because you said I could not go home," he answered.

I picked up the phone and called the emergency room of a nearby hospital. I told them I would be bringing in a teenager for treatment.

A nurse helped clean the Teardrop Kid's wound, and soon the doctor on call stitched the cut. The doctor had sewn a lot of cut human flesh in his career. He saw the tattooed teardrop underneath

Jose's right eye. He didn't ask him any questions but just sang a song while stitching him. It has been about twenty years since Jose was sewn, yet I still remember the doctor's song. He put words to the music of "When the Saints Go Marching In," singing as he stitched:

> When the teardrops get tattooed in,
> When the teardrops get tattooed in,
> I want to cry for all the gangsters,
> When the teardrops get tattooed in.

Jose tried not to cry, but the stitching was painful and real tears once again flowed over the tattoo. When the doctor finished his work, he gave the Teardrop Kid a little advice: "Son, life is full of problems. I became a doctor because I wanted to be part of life's solutions. I am not a perfect person. But it is a little more fun stitching than being stitched. Why don't you just listen to the people trying to help you?"

The Teardrop Kid didn't understand the doctor's advice. But he did remember the doctor calling him "son." He wanted badly to be someone's son.

After Jose left my group home he went back to his old neighborhood. He still got into trouble. For example, there was the time he noticed keys in the ignition of a car. He took the car for a ride and then brought the car back to where he had taken it. But he kept the keys. The next day he came back to take the car for another ride. As soon as he opened the door, he was grabbed by the owner who made a citizen's arrest and called the police. The police, as well as the owner of the car, remarked that the Teardrop Kid was a nice person. They did not understand why he thought he could take someone else's car and then return to try to take it a second time.

"Come on, son," said the policeman. "I've got to take you in."

The policeman put the handcuffs on Jose's wrists. "I notice you have some scars from stitches," remarked the officer. "I'm not hurting you, am I?"

The Teardrop Kid thought of the doctor in the emergency room. Like the cop, the doctor had called him "son." He began to cry. It wasn't from the pain of the handcuffs. It was from the pain of knowing he was still "part of the problem."

After the car theft, the Teardrop Kid spent a few months in the juvenile detention center. He did a lot of thinking about what the old doctor had told him. He made up his mind that he would try to be part of the solution. I was quite surprised a few years later when he called to tell me he had a job working in a group home helping other young men who had poor judgment. He seemed to enjoy his new role in life: being part of the solution.

Questions for Discussion

1. Are there pressures in your neighborhood or school to join a gang? If not yourself, do you know others who are under pressure? What help would you seek for yourself or others under such pressure? Discuss.

2. Describe someone you have know, perhaps yourself, who acted tough to cover up personal insecurity.

3. Have you ever tried to get adult attention in a silly way? Describe.

4. What are some communities doing to deal with gang violence in a positive and creative way?

A Butterfly on a Bald Man's Head

Sunnie was nine years old when she proclaimed herself to be a schoolteacher. Her "classroom" was the open field by her house. Her "students" were a squirrel, a jackrabbit, a prairie dog, and an occasional butterfly. Sometimes her own pet cat, Tabby, would show up for class. But Tabby would generally sleep while Sunnie recited all the stories she heard from her father at bedtime.

One day Sunnie's only student was Monarch the butterfly. Monarch came to class only about once every two weeks. Sunnie was happy to see him and began telling him the story of Cinderella. She told him of Cinderella's jealous stepsisters, the prince, and the great dance. But just as Sunnie reached the part about Cinderella leaving the party before midnight, Monarch flew off.

"Wait, don't fly away," cried Sunnie. "My story isn't finished yet."

Monarch wouldn't listen to Sunnie as she chased him through the field right onto the property of Mr. Simon Shadow. Sunnie did not even see the sign at the entrance of Mr. Shadow's driveway: No Trespassing. Carelessly, she ran right into Mr. Shadow as he was chopping wood in his back yard.

"Can't you read my sign?" screamed Mr. Shadow as he grabbed Sunnie by her right ear. Then Monarch the butterfly landed on his bald head. Sunnie, forgetting the pain in her ear, laughed because Mr. Shadow looked so silly. The old man did not think anything was funny. He warned Sunnie he would call the police the next time she came on his property.

Sunnie walked home with Monarch on her shoulder.

"See how you got me into trouble," she complained to the butterfly. "From now on you should stay in class and listen to my stories."

That evening Sunnie told her father about what happened at Mr. Shadow's house. He was very understanding and did not spank her for trespassing on Mr. Shadow's property. Instead he began to tell Sunnie a story that would teach her in a gentle way that it was dangerous to trespass.

"Once upon a time there was a little girl named Blondie who loved to chase butterflies. One day as Blondie was chasing a beautiful butterfly, she ran right into the house of the Three Bears, who had left their hot cereal on the table to cool."

At this point in her father's story, Sunnie said: "Daddy, let me continue with your story."

Sunnie's father was surprised but said, "Okay, you finish my story." This is how Sunnie told her father's story:

"Blondie did not try to taste the oatmeal of the Three Bears. And she did not try to sleep in their beds. Instead she cleaned their house and waited for them to come home. When the Bears came home, they were pleased to see her. They did not scold her for trespassing. They did not chase her out of their house. She did not fall and break her leg, like the famous Goldilocks. The Bears invited her to come back to their house the next day. Blondie accepted their invitation and came the next morning with

46

chocolate donuts. She knew the Bears were tired of the same old oatmeal, even though it was good for them."

Sunnie's father was amazed at the ending she gave to his story. He had tried to disguise the old Goldilocks story to teach that it was dangerous to trespass. Sunnie changed the story to show that people should be friendly. She also made a point that her father should buy some donuts once in a while instead of serving the same dull oatmeal every day for breakfast. Her father got the hint.

"Sunnie," said her dad, "let's buy some chocolate donuts tomorrow morning and bring them to Mr. Shadow. Nobody ever visits the old man except for little girls chasing butterflies. Sound like a good idea?"

"That's a great idea," answered Sunnie. "How did you think of such a thing?"

Sunnie's father smiled. They both went to sleep dreaming of chocolate donuts. The next morning they got up at the first crow of the rooster and went to the bakery to buy fresh donuts. They each ate one at the bakery, and they took two dozen with them. They went straight to Mr. Shadow's house. They knew he would be up early chopping wood. When they arrived in his back yard, Simon Shadow had a frown on his face. But when he saw the donuts, he smiled, probably for the first time in months.

"We want to share some of our donuts with you, Mr. Shadow," said Sunnie. "I did not mean to trespass or laugh at you yesterday. But one of my students was being impossible."

"One of your students?" asked Mr. Shadow with a question mark in his voice. He didn't know about the jackrabbit, the prairie dog, the squirrel, Tabby, and Monarch. So Sunnie told him more about her students and her classroom. He finally understood why she trespassed on his property while chasing

Monarch the butterfly. He apologized for his behavior toward her.

"I had no right to grab you by the ear, little girl. I apologize for my behavior yesterday. Thank you for the donuts."

A few tears came to Simon's eyes. And the three of them shook hands and promised to be friends. While they were saying good-bye, the jackrabbit, the squirrel, and the prairie dog, who had been hiding in the bushes, all begged for a donut.

"Are these your students?" asked Mr. Shadow as he gave each a donut.

"Yes," answered Sunnie. "These are all my students, except for Tabby who is probably sleeping and doesn't like chocolate anyway."

As she spoke Monarch the butterfly appeared and again landed on Mr. Shadow's bald head. This time he laughed.

After Sunnie and her dad left, Mr. Shadow took the No Trespassing sign down from his driveway and put up a sign that said: Welcome Friends. Before long, other children from the neighborhood came with their parents to visit him. He told the children many stories about his life. But their favorite was how a butterfly landed on his bald head and brought friendship to his home.

Questions for Discussion

1. The girl in the story acted out her fantasy of someday becoming a teacher. Do you know anyone who has acted out a fantasy?

2. Have you ever done a random act of kindness to a stranger just to be friendly and not expected a material reward? Describe.

3. Have you ever discovered kindness in someone you expected to be cruel? Describe.

4. Why does our society at the end of the twentieth century caution children from being friendly with strangers? Discuss the boundaries of being friendly with strangers.

A Shield of Feathers

Dawn, a poor widow, lived with a pet goose. The goose had no name. "Some day, I'll name my pet when she does something for people to remember," said the widow to her friends.

During her life as a farmworker, Dawn observed that geese protected their young. Since she was allergic to dogs and cats, she found a goose to be her perfect pet both for friendship and protection. As events turned out, her pet mother goose was given Italy's Presidential Medal of Honor. It was the first and only time in the history of Western Civilization that a goose was given a government's highest award. (Some wanted to make the goose a saint, but church leaders considered it too radical an idea.) You will find the widow's goose in the animal encyclopedia under the heading "geese greats" (should you wish to verify the historical facts behind this tale).

Because times were hard for poor widows, it came about that Dawn had to move from her little house to a one-room apartment. She could no longer pay rent for her little house with its garden and yard for her goose. It made Dawn very sad that she could not take her pet with her. She went to her neighbor, a young executive with bright red hair, named Suzie.

"Suzie, I have a pet goose. She needs a home and she would be a good pet for your son, Aaron."

Suzie was surprised by Dawn's request. She kept a very neat house and did not have the patience to clean up after a pet. She started to say: "I don't think so," when Dawn interrupted her.

"My goose would be a wonderful pet for your boy. Aaron would grow to love her. She would guard Aaron. She would be like an extra guardian angel, a real protector."

"I don't think it's a good idea," said Suzie. "I have heard that geese can be pretty nasty and have a mean bite. Aaron gets nervous when mosquitoes bite him. He wouldn't relate to a goose."

"Trust me," said Dawn. "My goose is not wild. She will love and protect Aaron."

At this point Aaron came into the room where the two women were talking and he begged his mother to let him have the goose. Suzie wanted to say no. But when she looked into her son's pleading eyes, she said: "Well, maybe it will be all right on a trial basis."

An agreement was reached. The widow Dawn left her pet with Suzie and Aaron. Then she moved to her little apartment. Within an hour the goose followed the child everywhere he went.

For the next two weeks everything went smoothly for Suzie, Aaron, and his new pet. Then on a Monday morning, as Barney the mailman was walking down the street, a vicious pit bull named Beelzebub leaped out of his yard to attack him. The dog belonged to a Mr. Smithwesson who lived on the same street.

Fortunately, the postman got into his car before the dog attacked him, and he managed to phone the police.

"There's a mad dog here in the neighborhood. He nearly got me. He is heading for the house where there lives a little boy named Aaron. I can see the boy in his yard, playing with his pet goose. Send a car here quickly. That dog needs to be tranquilized and captured before he hurts someone."

Beelzebub entered Aaron's yard. White liquid was dripping from his mouth. The goose sensed the danger and spread her wings over Aaron, who was frozen with fear. She made the first move and snapped at the dog. Beelzebub, snarling and drooling, attacked the defiant goose. Feathers were flying as the valiant goose fought back. There was blood and Beelzebub went crazy. Two minutes had passed since the mailman phoned for help. The sirens of police cars could be heard in the distance. Barney the mailman left his car, ran to the yard, jumped the fence, and tackled Beelzebub just as he put his jaws on the goose's throat. Barney had the mad dog pinned to the ground when the officer from animal control shot Beelzebub with a tranquilizer. The dog fell limp. The goose still had her wings spread out protecting Aaron.

With the animal control officer came Dina, a young veterinarian who immediately attended to the goose's neck wounds. She had never given first aid to a goose before, so she was understandably a little nervous. After bandaging the goose, Dina gave a big hug to Aaron, who was still shivering from fear. It was at this point that Aaron's mom arrived home with Dawn.

To say the very least, the women were shocked at the feathers, the blood, the police cars, and the tranquilized Beelzebub. Suzie ran to embrace Aaron and Dawn knelt beside her beloved pet.

"I'm so glad you're alive," the women said in unison.

That evening Suzie and Dawn held a party. Among the people who came were Barney the mailman, Dina the veterinarian, and even Mr. Smithwesson, who apologized to everyone for keeping such a vicious dog. He had built a fancy dog house for Beelzebub, which he said he would turn into a playhouse for Aaron and his courageous pet.

The widow Dawn brought out a cake with two candles, one for Aaron and one for the goose. She called it a friendship cake. Since the goose couldn't eat cake, she gave her some carrot juice.

Before Aaron blew out the candles, everyone made their wishes. Aaron made his out loud: "I wish that Dawn could live in our house." His mother and the widow smiled a "yes" to each other.

"No trial basis for you, Dawn," said Suzie.

Aaron had his wish. Everyone clapped, even the bandaged goose with her wings brushing across Aaron's happy face.

Aaron and Dawn finally named their goose. They chose "Pro" because she was both a protector and a professional.

Questions for Discussion

1. Do you have a pet? What are the benefits and responsibilities of having a pet?

2. Share an example of how your pet or some other animal has shown what we call "human qualities."

3. Would you have a pet who was trained to attack? If so, what kind of precautions would you have to take to avoid attack of the innocent?

4. Discuss any films you have seen which illustrate the loyalty of animals to humans.

Dressing for Survival

Once there were two little girls, sisters, who liked to dress as grownups. They had a brother, age five, and the three played a game they called "House." The game was easy to play. They took turns playing "father," "mother," and "child." The sisters often dressed up as "father" and "mother." Their brother played himself. However, one day his sisters decided he should play "mother" and dressed him like a girl. Besides putting him in a dress, they tied a ribbon in his hair and put lipstick on his lips. "If he is to be our mother, he must look like a woman," reasoned his sisters. The sisters did a good job with the costume. They made their brother look like a girl.

As fate would have it, the day the boy was dressed as a girl his father walked into the room. He was a retired navy man who devoted much of his life to body building. His appearance was very rugged, with tattoos of monsters and snakes on his forearms. He wanted his son to be macho like him. So you can imagine his thoughts and feelings when he saw his son dressed like a girl.

"What the Sam Hill are ye doing with a dress on? Get that girl's paint off your face before I make ye walk the plank." ("Walk the plank" was the old sailor's way of saying, "I will spank you.") "Unless

56

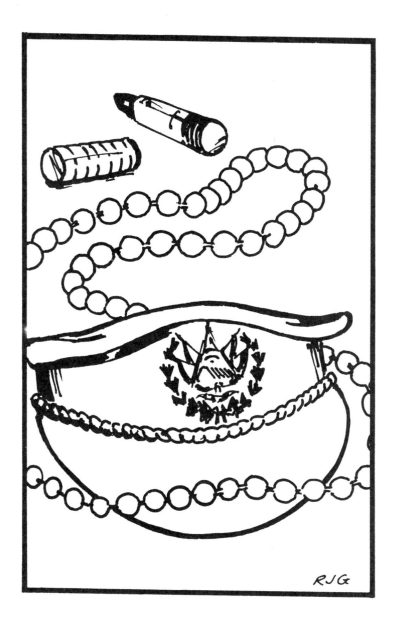

you're a Scotsman playing a bagpipe, ye don't wear a skirt."

The father asked his son to promise never to wear girls' clothes ever again. The son was ashamed. He promised.

The children continued to play house, but from that day forward they obeyed their father's wishes. The boy wore his own clothes at all times.

It happened one day that the children's father got into an argument with the army general who threw out his nation's president and became a dictator. This general, before entering the military, had been a TV wrestler with the ring name of "Pale Pig." Now General Pale Pig was putting innocent people into jail. The children's father challenged General Pale Pig to restore democracy to their country. He had fought for his country so that his children could live in freedom. The Pale Pig was a greedy and prejudiced man. His soldiers killed a lot of people who resisted him. He did not care about the lives of those he put in jail.

After a long argument, the Pale Pig directed his soldiers to handcuff the old sailor with the tattooed arms. They put him in a harsh jail. After a few months, he died from the bad treatment.

As the boy and his sisters grew up, they told everyone about the Pale Pig and how their father died in his jail. The Pale Pig found out the children were talking about him. He became very angry. He brought false charges against the old sailor's boy, now seventeen, and jailed him in the same cell where his father died of starvation and neglect.

"I will make an example of this young man for all to see. I will keep him in jail until he rots," bragged the Pale Pig.

After the young man had been in jail a few days, a guard came to bring him a piece of stale bread. He recognized the young man as a former classmate. He felt sorry for his old friend. He knew his classmate would be put to death.

"The evil man is going to let you die," said the guard. "I will try to help you, but I need your ideas. I will come back to see you tomorrow."

That night the young man lay awake trying to think of how the guard could help him escape. He had once seen a movie about how a man broke out of jail by using a saw to cut through the bars of the cell. The saw had been smuggled into the jail in a cake. However, in the Pale Pig's jail no one was allowed to bring in cakes.

That evening as the young man was falling asleep, he remembered the day his father scolded him and his sisters for dressing him up like a girl. He sat up on his bed thinking. That old memory gave him an idea. He would tell his idea to the guard when he came to see him the next day.

When his old school buddy, the guard, came into his cell, he told him about his idea.

"You can get me out of here if you are willing to take the risk. Just get me some girls' clothes and a razor. I will shave my face and put on some powder and lipstick. If anyone questions you, just tell them I am your girlfriend. Of course, it will be discovered by others that I am gone. You will be blamed. Are you sure you want to take this risk for me? You could get killed."

The guard thought about the risk. He did not like his job of having to keep innocent people in jail. He decided to take the risk. The next day he brought a razor, a wig, and his sister's clothes and lipstick to the jail. He gave the package to the young man. Quickly and quietly the young man shaved, dressed, and put on the makeup and wig. He thought of the time his sisters had dressed him to look like a girl. He thought of how angry his father was with him, how he promised never again to dress like a girl.

The guard came to his cell. "Are you ready?" he whispered.

"Let's get out of here," answered the young man, now looking like the guard's girlfriend.

The two young men walked arm in arm out of the jail. The other guards thought the young man was the guard's girlfriend. They did not suspect an escape.

Once outside the jail, both the guard and the young man got into a taxi and went straight to the dock where the two sisters had hired a boat to take them out of the country.

"Do you like my dress?" he asked his sisters.

"You're kind of cute," they smiled as they walked onto the boat that would take them to freedom. "I think even our dad is smiling now."

The brother, the guard, and the two sisters made it to the open sea. Strangely enough, it was a tough-looking sailor with many tattoos who helped them onto a foreign rescue ship as their little sailboat was about to sink. The brother and his sisters looked at each other. Each knew what the others were thinking. Their dad was not only smiling. Somehow he was still involved in their lives.

The story of the brother and his two sisters did not end with their rescue at sea. They learned the language of the country that gave them shelter, and devoted their lives to restoring the freedom that the Pale Pig had stolen from their country.

Questions for Discussion

1. Describe some of the things you have done to make a parent or guardian proud of you.

2. The dad wanted his son to be "macho," all "man." How did the influence of his sisters help him to become an intelligent and brave man? Can you give

examples of how feminine influence has made a boy you know more "manly"?

3. Have you ever taken a personal risk for someone? Describe.

4. This story took place in Haiti in 1992. Can you point to Haiti on a map? Do you know anything about the history or culture of its people that is related to U.S. history and culture?

Miss Figgie and Sam

In olden days when trees had names, there was a pine named Sam who lived in the back yard of a family home where children played in his shade. Boys and girls came from the neighborhood to climb and swing from Sam's branches. On hot summer days the old folks slept in his shade. In winter, neighbors collected his cones to decorate their homes or burn in their fireplaces. Sam was a contented tree because he made so many others happy. However, one of his neighbor trees was not happy. Her name was Miss Figgie. She had just completed her first season in the back yard.

In the language that only trees understand, Miss Figgie complained to Sam: "Your branches and roots are getting too close to me. I don't want to be touched. Stay away from me."

Sam was upset with the message from Miss Figgie. Yet, he answered like a kind uncle: "Don't worry, my little one. The gardener hired by the family will trim my branches if they touch you. Our roots will probably touch. There is nothing we can do about that. Since the days of the very first trees, roots have tangled with roots. But don't worry. Roots know how to share space."

Miss Figgie was not happy with Sam's explanation.

"First of all, Mister Sam Pine Tree, I am not your so-called 'little one.' I belong to the royal Fig Family,

which traces its beginnings to the Garden of Eden. I am of royal sap. I want most of this yard for myself. I deserve it because I give sugar treats and all you give are dry cones and tasteless needles. I don't want to share root space with you. What I really want is for you to get away from me, even if it means your falling over and dying."

Sam had not heard this kind of talk even from the children when they got in fights with each other. He wondered why Miss Figgie wanted him to fall over and die. His roots would not hurt her. Once again he tried to calm her.

"My dear Miss Figgie, please listen. There is room for both of us in this yard. Do not be jealous or upset because you are different from me. The Great Gardener also made the Rainbow of many colors. Blue does not say to Purple, 'Get away from me,' but rejoices to have a friend next to her. Yellow does not say to Orange, 'Get away, you're touching me,' but is happy to have a neighbor. I am your neighbor. Loosen up. We have to share. That's the way it is."

Miss Figgie did not want Sam's advice. She talked back.

"Don't preach to me, Mister Know-It-All. Remember that the very first people covered themselves with fig leaves before there was cotton or wool. You don't read that they used pine needles or anything you or your ancestors had to offer. You are only good for wood to be used for fires."

Sam had received vibrations from many trees during his lifetime. But he never heard anything like the anger that vibrated from Miss Figgie's fragile branches. He could not understand how a creature that produced fruit as sweet as candy could be so bitter about him. He decided to ignore her.

Days passed in silence. When the cold of winter came, Miss Figgie lost all her leaves while Sam looked more handsome than ever. Then the family gardener came with his pruning saw. He did not touch Sam, but he cut off most of Miss Figgie's branches. She was furious. She broke her silence with Sam.

"Look what they have done to me! All my branches are cut! Look at yourself. The gardener did not even touch you! It's not fair! I look ugly!"

The cool mist of morning resembled tears, which rolled off Sam's mighty branches onto Miss Figgie.

For the first time Sam felt sorry for her. A gentle wind arose and he leaned over her, like a hen broods over her chicks. Sam felt strong and protective. He knew his little neighbor was hurting. What could she know of the laws of the garden? Could she understand why it was so important to cut branches from the fig and not from the pine?

"My little sister, the family gardener did not cut your branches to make you ugly but to make you more beautiful than ever. In the springtime your branches will be stronger than before and your fruit more plentiful and sweet. Believe me. That's the way of the garden."

Miss Figgie went into a long sleep. She became aware that her roots were touching those of Sam. He seemed to give her strength. Winter passed into springtime and her pruned branches sprouted out anew and bore the sweetest fruit. The old people came to her in June and then again in August saying things like: "I have never seen figs so big and beautiful."

At summer's end, Miss Figgie figured out that Sam really was her friend and not her enemy. The gardener remarked to the children: "It seems that fig tree is leaning toward the pine." The children answered as children often do: "Miss Figgie is in love with Sam."

Just then two branches from the fig tree waved in a gust of wind. The same wind caught Sam, and gently pushed him to touch Miss Figgie. The gardener smiled and said to himself: "Kids are really smart these days."

Questions for Discussion

1. What are the qualities in yourself or in friends that you find valuable?

2. Why was Miss Figgie valuable? What was wrong in her thinking?

3. What qualities of value did Sam illustrate?

4. How does the symbolism of pruning a tree or vine carry over into the area of human behavior? Do people need to be pruned? Explain.

A Rematch Made in Heaven

F rank was a young man who lived in a foster home. His favorite hobby was watching professional wrestling on TV. He knew most of the TV wrestlers by name and had autographed pictures of muscle men lining the walls of his room. His foster parents catered to his interest in wrestlers by giving him outfits (capes, masks, tights, etc.) resembling those of his favorite TV wrestlers.

Frank's foster parents were not themselves interested in big-time wrestling. They were college professors who collected many works of art from around the world, which they had in their home. One of their pieces of art was a painting of two of history's most famous men: David and Goliath. Frank was curious about the picture, which depicted a young man unarmed except for a slingshot up against a heavily armed man described as a giant. One night before bedtime, he asked Bob, his foster father, to tell him about the two warriors in the picture.

"Frank," explained Bob, "this is not exactly a bedtime story. But I think you are old enough to understand it. Once there were two groups of people who were not getting along with each other. One group was known as the Philistines, or Phillies for short. The other one was called the Israelites, or Lights. The Phillies and Lights had been fighting each other in a kind of hit-and-run guerrilla war for many days.

"It happened one day that the biggest, meanest warrior of the Phillies, Goliath, challenged the Lights. He called out: 'If you can beat me, my people will be your slaves. But if I win, you will be our slaves. Send out your best man to fight me.'

"Goliath wanted to take on the best warrior Israel could offer. Many gathered that day to watch the battle. But who would fight for the Lights? They had no giants. The big man, Goliath, with his suit of bronze and his massive spear, put fear in the hearts of all. This was something different from big-time wrestling as we know it, Frank. It was not play acting. They really fought to kill.

"The best warriors for the Lights began making excuses about why they couldn't go out and take the giant's challenge. Goliath's laugh could be heard for miles. He ridiculed his enemies and called them names like 'sissies' and 'wimps.' Because of his size and strength, he was certain that he could beat anyone.

"At this point a young boy named David answered the challenge of Goliath. His only weapon was a homemade slingshot, and he carried five smooth rocks. Upon seeing the young man armed with only a slingshot, Goliath laughed all the louder.

"'Am I a dog, that this boy comes to chase me with sticks?'

"As Goliath's laugh subsided, the two men stared at each other. The soldiers on both sides were silent. David said nothing as he put a rock into his sling. Before Goliath had a chance to say 'Jiminy Cricket,' David felled him with a shot to his forehead. Goliath's fall shook the earth like a mild earthquake. David then took the giant's sword and cut off his head. It was bloody. This is no children's story, for sure. All wars are disgusting and bloody. The Phillies ran

away in panic. The Lights ruled the neighborhood and they made David their king."

Frank thanked his foster father for telling him the story, but he really did not like the ending. Frank had seen so much violence in his own family that he was bothered by people beating up on each other. He loved to watch big-time wrestling on TV because he knew it was fake. He knew that the wrestlers got together before their matches to rehearse their script for a fixed fight.

That night Frank had a dream that gave him an idea for a better ending to the story of David and Goliath. In his dream he was in a locker room that belonged to the world of those who had lived in the past. In the locker room he overheard a conversation between two men he recognized as being from the painting in his foster parents' home: David and Goliath. The two famous warriors of the past were talking about their big fight and all the people who died in the war. This is how Frank explained his dream the next day:

"In my dream, I told David and Goliath they should have gotten together before their fight. I told Goliath he should have faked a fall and walked off limping. He could have proclaimed David the winner but then challenged him to a rematch the following week. Wrestling fans love rematches. They hold your interest. I told the two of them that no one had to die, that people wanted entertainment and not the death and destruction of real war."

Bob asked Frank: "Did the two warriors in your dream agree with you?"

"They sure did," answered Frank. "They liked my idea so much, they decided to put on exhibition matches for all the Phillies and Lights in the great stadium where they now live."

"Were they going to fix their matches?" asked Bob.

"Yes. Goliath was to win the first match, just to stimulate interest. After that they would trade off winning and losing."

"You have an interesting imagination, Frank," remarked his foster dad.

That evening Frank and Bob sat down with a big bowl of popcorn to watch an old film of a match between two TV warriors, Gorgeous George and Baron Leone.

Foster father and son agreed that show business battles made more sense than real wars.

Questions for Discussion

1. Are you like Frank in the sense you are bothered by people who beat up on each other in real life?

2. What are some examples of the violence of everyday life that affect you directly or indirectly? Discuss how violence affects everyone in our country, at least indirectly.

3. What organized sports, in your opinion, cross the line between sport and brutality?

4. Research Project: Look up in an art book some of the classic paintings and sculptures of David.

Cicero Learns to Speak

Miss Wonder, an eighth-grade teacher, decided to have an essay contest for her students. The winner was to receive the prize of a trip to Disneyland. The essay could be truth or fiction. Miss Wonder decided the winner would be "the one who moves my heart with a human interest story."

The student with the highest grades in Miss Wonder's class was a boy named Cicero. The students called him "Computer" or "The Brain." He always boasted of his 4.0 grade average. He was favored to win the contest because many of the other students were children of immigrants struggling to learn basic English.

Cicero entered the contest with a science fiction story. He showed it to many of the students before turning it in to Miss Wonder. Everyone liked it. Here is a sample of his story:

"In the year five million B.C. (give or take a million years), some creatures from the planet 'Studebaker' (galaxy unknown) arrived on planet Earth. They landed in South America and found there a peace-loving people who led a simple life hunting and fishing. The Studebakers, as they insisted on being called, had many more words than the Earthlings. They were very good with words and talked the Earthlings out of most of their food. They also brought with them rare diseases from the planet

Studebaker. Soon all the Earthlings died except for Max, a hermit who only left his cave to search for food."

Cicero's essay went on to describe the strange ways of the Studebakers, how they began to use fossil fuels until the Earth's atmosphere as it was known millions of years ago was destroyed. He described the meeting of Max and Sunbeam, the daughter of the Studebaker chieftain. (Their offspring gave rise to modern humans.) By the time he was done with his essay, Cicero had written a small book. Students in Miss Wonder's class were heard to say: "How can we compete with Cicero, who has so many words?"

The long-awaited day finally came when the winner of Miss Wonder's essay contest was to be announced. Miss Wonder did not give the name of the winner. Instead she read the winning essay to her class. It went like this:

"I was six years old. A bad thing happened to my family. My father and mother wake me in middle of night. They very afraid. They tell me to hurry and get dressed. Then we walk to ocean. We get on boat. There not much room to sit or stand because too many people. We sit, no moving. We all afraid. We told not to cry or make noise. The captain of boat start motor. We go out to the water. Tears in my father's eyes. He never cry before.

"We on water two days. Then motor stop. Men work to start motor. Motor is dead. The sun is very hot. Children cry. They thirsty. Not very much food. Some fishermen come to us. We very happy. Maybe they help us. But no. Fishermen very evil. They have guns. They take our money. They kill people. They throw people in ocean. Many people die in water. My mother sees box floating in water. We hold on to box. Box saves our lives. My mother says: 'Angel send box.' My father and brothers not so lucky. They die in water.

74

"We float with angel box three days. Then people on beach see us. They take us to their home. They give us food."

When Miss Wonder finished reading the winning essay, some students had tears in their eyes. But Cicero was red with anger. He was not a good loser. Miss Wonder announced the winner, a girl named Thua who had been in the United States only two years. Thua was surprised and embarrassed. She said to Miss Wonder: "Maybe I do not deserve to win. I do not have many words."

Without asking permission to talk, Cicero stood up and said: "Miss Wonder, Thua is right. I do have a better command of the language. After all, this is an English class. Why does a foreigner win? English is not even her main language. She doesn't even know how to write the past tense, not to mention the past perfect or the conditional. She doesn't use articles. Her essay is primitive."

Many in the class were angry with Cicero's remarks. Arthur stood up and called him "Fathead." Miss Wonder told everyone to be quiet. Then she spoke to Cicero.

"Cicero, you are an excellent student. I have never given you less than an A. You deserve recognition for your accomplishments. But in this case, Thua wrote an essay in which she told us of the life and death issues of her life. This does not mean that yours was not good. You have won many prizes and you will continue to win more. Thua with her limited English spent hours struggling to tell her story, which, according to my rules, was best. She moved my heart and enlightened all the students. Please be a gentleman. You do not always have to win."

Cicero knew that the eyes of the class were on him. He turned to Thua and apologized. Then he turned to Miss Wonder and made a request.

"I have saved my money for two years in order to someday go to Disneyland. If it is all right with my parents, may I go along with you and her, even though I did not win? I could help her learn new words. She could teach me about her native language."

Miss Wonder was quite pleased with Cicero's request. She told the class that Cicero's change of attitude was something like the miracle box that saved Thua and her mother. Everyone in the class agreed with Miss Wonder, even Arthur.

Cicero went to Disneyland with Thua and Miss Wonder. He learned to say many words in Thua's language. He also learned a little more about foreign cultures and a lot more about himself.

Questions for Discussion

1. Was the teacher really fair to Cicero? Do you think he was a "fathead"? What valid point might he have had in his complaint if he presented it differently?

2. Have you ever felt cheated because someone you thought a lesser student got a better grade than you? Explain the circumstance.

3. If you were the teacher in this story, what rules would you have made for the contest?

4. How many ethnic groups, including tribal Native American nations, can you identify in the United States? What national origin identifies your ancestors?

Gum Up My Nose

Every human being has the opportunity to learn survival from personal experience. The following are a few stories of survival from my own childhood and adolescence.

When I was four years old I learned that an adult could knock me out if I did not cooperate. Here is what happened.

I was innocently riding my tricycle in the back yard of our family home. Being a coordinated child, I was simultaneously chewing gum while riding my tricycle in circles on the cement. Then for some unknown reason, I put the gum from my mouth firmly up my nasal passage. I thought nothing of my achievement and kept on riding in circles. Eventually my mother saw what I had done and became quite alarmed when I would not allow her to remove the gum from inside my nose. Her decision was to take me to a clinic to have the gum removed by a nurse.

The year was 1937. I am not sure what the rules were in medical clinics for cases such as mine. The nurse who attended me had little patience when I would not allow her to touch me. After a brief encounter in which she scratched me and I scratched her, she put a cloth over my face. I went unconscious. Later I was told the towel had chloroform on it. I have not been chloroformed since.

Three years later my interests expanded from tricycle riding to the reading of comic books. In those pre-TV days of radio, our fledgling minds were not saturated with violence and the antics of movie stuntmen. We relied on Superman and Batman comics to stimulate our imaginations. After reading how Superman flew so easily, I climbed the tree in front of our house with a makeshift cape to practice "flying." The outcome of my adventure was hardly heroic. My pants got caught on a branch. I was literally hanging upside down, more like a bat, than any comic book superhero. My mother rescued me by cutting me loose.

Another survival experience took place at a lake named "Shangrila," which to this day I cannot find on a map. But I know it existed in Southern California. I was about ten years old and had not yet learned how to swim. A friend named Gerald invited me to cut school and join him at Shangrila. I recall walking into the lake up to my waist. My next step put me beneath the surface of the water. I was struggling to fight my way to the top and was able to grab on to a kind of floating dock. I understood for the first time the fine line between life and death. I took swimming lessons after that.

Another near-death experience took place while on a Boy Scout outing. I was hiking with my scout leader and a few other boys in a mountain area. At one point we came to a very steep climb where there was a kind of mechanical lift, an old abandoned skeleton of a tram for sightseers. The boy ahead of me on the climb unintentionally kicked loose a large boulder, which narrowly missed my head as it sailed down the mountain. As I write this story fifty years later, I can still sense the velocity of that rock whizzing past my head.

During my high school years there were other close encounters, now related to cars. My school had no

public transportation, and I often had to rely on hitchhiking as my main means of transportation. One day I took a ride with a man who recklessly passed the car in front of his, going over the double line on a blind curve. His car was a 1938 Ford. On the other side of the double line, coming straight at us, was a 1941 Packard sedan. My driver swerved back in time to avoid a head-on collision, but the Packard hit the rear of our car. We spun around but landed safely. Most of the damage happened to the Packard. No one was hurt. After that I decided to ride my bicycle the six miles to school until I got a car my senior year.

These are some of my survival stories. To this very day I do not try to fly like Superman or climb dangerous rocks or hitchhike or even stick gum up my nose.

Questions for Discussion

1. Have you ever had an experience in which you came close to having a serious injury or even dying? Describe.

2. What have your experiences of "close calls" taught you?

3. Why is hitch-hiking more dangerous today than it was in the author's youth?

4. Name some people who have used their own close encounters with death to promote a better life for others.

Summer Camp Brat

When I was ten years old, I went to a summer camp for two weeks. It was there that I met another ten-year-old who would make a lasting impression on me. It was the first time I had been away from my own home. I saw a mountain lake for the first time and experienced a little creature called a tick who likes to bury itself in your skin. I saw a rattlesnake for the first time, and I had my first encounter with an unusual species of human brat.

For us city boys, camp was a chance to experience living in a tent, using an "outhouse" instead of a flushing toilet, singing silly camp songs such as "Ninety-Nine Bottles of Beer on the Wall," hiking on hot dusty trails, and eating a lot of what was called bread pudding. We campers learned about poison oak and all the little things in nature that said "Beware." Besides being new to the beautiful sights and smells of the mountains not available in the city, we campers were on the first day total strangers to each other.

After a few days of getting used to camp life, the young adult in charge of us, a Native American named Joaquin, took ten of us on a hike. We had not gone too far when Joaquin spotted a rattlesnake. He told us all to stand back. Then with a stick he propelled the snake from our trail. I realized our lives were in the hands of our guide.

A few miles farther down the trail, Joaquin's ability was again challenged. This time the test did not come from a poisonous reptile but from one of the campers.

It had been a hot day. Most of us were out-of-shape, soft, baby-fat "city boys." The boy I will refer to as Superbrat was, like the rest of us, tired. He sat on the trail and refused to go another step. Joaquin told him he had to keep going. But he cried like a baby. I was tired too, but crying was out of the question. The rattlesnake was easy for Joaquin to control, but he could not take a stick and fling Superbrat off the trail. So he simply took him by the hand and dragged him along for the rest of the hike. It was on that hike that Joaquin taught us that dealing with a poisonous snake was a lot easier than dealing with a crying, resistant child.

All of us campers survived the five-mile hike. I do not remember Joaquin being mean to Superbrat. He just wanted to help him grow up. Then something happened a few days later which pushed everyone's patience to the limit.

A group of us was on the camp's playing field. A wire fence separated our field from a public road below. It was about four in the afternoon and we were standing around waiting for dinner. A group of young people, African Americans, walked down the road alongside the fence. (There was a lot of segregation in those days. We were in an all-white camp and they were from an all-black camp.) They were minding their own business, just walking from the lake to their camp, when it happened.

Superbrat yelled out the "n" word. The young people heard him but did not react. They kept on walking as though they did not hear it. Superbrat was smiling and thinking he was a big shot. All I could think of at the moment was his screaming and crying on the trail a few days before.

A few minutes later, some of the angry boys returned. They began throwing rocks at us. Superbrat's problem was now our problem. He was like the rattlesnake that needed to be propelled off the trail. He was full of poison. I thought we might die because of him. Where was Joaquin?

When Joaquin saw the rocks flying, he came running to the scene. The angry young men retreated. We told Joaquin what had happened. He grabbed Superbrat by the arm. I think he wanted to twist it very hard. But he stayed calm and announced: "Tomorrow we will go on a ten-mile hike."

We all went on that hike. It was a hot day and everyone was uncomfortable. We were waiting for Superbrat to cry and carry on like he did on the five-mile hike. We saw pain on his face and tears in his eyes, but he kept on going.

When we reached the halfway point of the hike, we were quite surprised to see the young people from the all-black camp. With a little help from Joaquin, Superbrat apologized for his stupid hate word. The young people accepted his apology.

Superbrat was an angel for the remaining days of camp. I often wondered what happened to him as he grew to be an adult. I would like to think he never again used a racist word or instigated trouble. I have often thought about Joaquin, how he taught us to respect nature and to recognize which plants and reptiles were poisonous. Most of all, I think about how he showed us that it is possible to remove the poison in the human subspecies of "racist brat."

Questions for Discussion

1. Can you think of someone like Joaquin, a person outside your immediate family who helped you grow as a person? How did this person help you?

2. Have you known someone like Superbrat? Did he or she ever change?

3. Have you ever been in the presence of a person who used racially offensive words or told a distasteful ethnic joke? How did you react? If you did nothing, what did you want to do?

4. Explain why racism is compared to a poison. Is it a good comparison?

My Grammar School Hero

Nick burned himself into my memory. In the 1940s, Nick and I attended All Souls, a Catholic grammar school in Alhambra, California. All of our teachers were religious sisters. They not only taught us the academic subjects but encouraged us to be good people. They read us stories about saints, the heroes and heroines who gave up their own personal comfort to benefit the downtrodden of the world. The sisters made a point of encouraging the boys to consider becoming priests. They told me I should become a priest. But not Nick.

In the classroom Nick was not a problem. He sat at his desk and minded his own business. He did not pull the hair of the girl in the desk in front of him or throw spit wads when the sister's back was turned. But class was boring for Nick. Recess and noon lunch hour were his times of achievement. In class he simply put his head on his desk and closed his eyes. This is why the sisters did not consider him material for the priesthood.

It was outside the classroom that I best remember Nick. Recess came at ten a.m., after we had been in the classroom for two hours. Then Nick did what he did best—his imitation of a World War II plane called a "Zero." In movies about that war, the Japanese pilots were portrayed by Hollywood actors grinning and wearing wire rim glasses, diving at their targets

before releasing their bombs. Sometimes the planes went directly into their targets and were called "kamikazes" or suicide bombers.

Nick wore wire rim glasses and grinned like the actors. The amazing thing about his acting ability was the way he could put his whole person into the world of aerial war. He himself was both plane and pilot. Stretching his arms in the form of wings, he ran around the school yard making noises like a plane engine. Then at a given moment he would aim himself in the direction of another student and often take a dive onto the ground. There was no soft, grassy lawn in our school yard but hard dirt. Nick acquired many scratches and bruises with his dive bombing. Once he broke his glasses. After every recess he was dirty, sweaty, and sometimes bloody. Nick was not an honor student, but he was probably the best one-man aerial show ever produced by a grammar school.

The sisters did not interfere with Nick's need to be a pilot. Dive bombing was his way of getting rid of his excess energy so that he could sit still in class.

While Nick was fighting in World War II as a Japanese pilot in the school yard, he also had to join us in our marching drills. The nephew of our pastor, John, taught us to march, salute, and do various military drills: about face, company halt, forward march. It was from John that Nick and I learned the word "yardbird." (It was a military word that I believe meant "dimwit," by the way John used it.) John often called Nick a yardbird because he purposely marched out of step or kept going straight when commanded "about face." John's face would turn red in yelling at Nick. He didn't know Nick as his classmates did, as an "enemy pilot."

Nick and I belonged to the same Boy Scout patrol. One day five of us put on our uniforms complete with our scout knives and went out into the hills of East Los Angeles. Our purpose was to prepare a meal as a

requirement to become "second-class scouts." We
were to dig a hole, bury potatoes, burn some wood,
and allow the coals to cook the buried potatoes. (In
those days it was legal to build fires in the hills
surrounding residential areas).

The smoke from our fires attracted the attention of
some young boys from the other side of the hills.
There were six of them. At first they were friendly
and asked to see our knives. We showed them our
knives, which they immediately took and then used to
threaten us. We were very innocent and naive and it
took us a while to realize that we were being held up.
The boys searched our pockets.

No one in our patrol said anything as the youngest
of the boys began searching us. As the search went on
at knifepoint, two of the boys saw an orange on the
ground near Nick's feet. They both took a dive for the
orange. In doing so, one of the boys cut Nick's hand.
We had all seen blood on Nick before, but nothing like
this. The cut was deep. Nick did not blink. It was as
though he was a hardened war veteran. He did not
cry. The young gangsters who held us up suddenly
departed with our knives. Maybe they were scared by
the accidental cutting.

As we walked back to our own neighborhood, we all
realized we were very lucky. We knew that there
could have been more injuries. Nick did not get a
chance to cook his potatoes. But he did pass a
different kind of self-test for discipline and keeping
cool under pressure. Maybe he was prepared for that
moment by all his training as a Japanese pilot in the
yard of All Souls School.

None of us told the sisters, the pastor's nephew, or
even our own parents about what happened in the
hills of East Los Angeles that day when we set out to
cook our underground potatoes. When Nick's hand
healed, he continued to do his aerial exercises in the
school yard.

World War II came to an end the summer before seventh grade. With an end to the real war came an end to Nick's schoolyard bombing. We later went to different high schools and I lost track of Nick. I don't know if he indeed became a priest, a pilot, a policeman, or none of the above. But I do know that my memories of him have never faded. He is my grade school hero.

Suggestions for Discussion

1. Were you ever threatened with violence in grade school? How did you handle the situation? On reflection, is there anything you would have done differently?

2. Who do you look upon as a hero among your own peer group? What are the qualities you like in a person?

3. What detail in the scenario of the holdup and knifing of Nick suggests that some gang violence may be related to poverty?

4. Many of the Hollywood films made during wartime made the enemy look like cartoon characters. Have you seen such a film? Why is the enemy military purposely portrayed to look odd or stupid?

Nose Breaker

You always remember those who break your
bones. This is why I remember Don, my high
school friend. In a way he was like Nick from the
previous story: fearless, loyal, and entertaining.
Whereas Nick presented himself as a Japanese
fighter pilot, Don fancied himself a steamroller.

My first recollection of Don was in freshman
algebra class. Our school, Cantwell High, was in East
Los Angeles. It was a new school with the Christian
Brothers of Ireland as its teachers and
administrators. Our algebra teacher was Brother
Reagan, a smiling Irishman dedicated to making men
of us "soft California kids." (The brothers were from
the Midwest and East Coast, where boys were better
students and tougher athletes.) Each day as Brother
Reagan walked by Don's desk to check his homework,
he would give him a solid punch on his shoulder. It
was a friendly hit, in the days when there could be
some normal physical contact in the classroom
without fear of a lawsuit. Don always smiled when
hit by the brother. Both were built like apes. Looking
back, Algebra 1 was more like "primate playtime."

Though he was quiet in class, Don was talkative
during the noon lunch hour. He was always
surrounded by friends, who were entertained by his
stories and comments. He was like a philosopher
surrounded by disciples. His lunch consisted of raw

vegetables and fruits. Sometimes he would simply eat
a head of cabbage for lunch. This was in a time before
vegetarianism was popular.

The bone that Don broke, or that I broke on him,
was my nose. It happened during football practice.
We were doing punt returns on a hot, dusty field.
(Our coach didn't want us to spoil the grass so we
practiced on dirt.) Don was returning punts and my
job was to tag him. What I did not know about Don at
the time was the fact that he never tried to avoid a
tackler. His style was simply to run over anyone in
his way. With what seemed the force of a locomotive,
he ran over me. My bloodied face simply drew a smile
from our coach, Mr. K., who, like Brother Reagan,
dedicated his life to toughening up soft California
kids. In his college years playing for UCLA, Don
learned to avoid tacklers. But during his high school
days he ate up opponents like they were so many
heads of cabbage.

I didn't enjoy football. The thought of practices
depressed me. Coach K. often told us the story about
Ray Jones, one of his high school players, who showed
no emotion when he had several of his teeth knocked
out during a practice. That toothless player was held
up as an ideal for us. (This was at a time before there
were obligatory face guards.) We were encouraged to
take mutilation without showing emotion or else we
would spend the rest of our lives as soft California
kids. Not becoming tough was the ultimate evil in the
mind of our coach. He began to like me after I lost a
front tooth during one game.

Don did not like the coach. He was already tough
and didn't need what he called "stupid Ray Jones
stories."

I really did not enjoy conditioning or practices on
dusty fields in the smog of East Los Angeles. But I
looked upon football as a necessary initiation into
manhood. It was a way of proving to my friends I was

not a sissy. The coach made me do what I would not have done on my own. Yet it was Don who really, in a sense, did more for us than the coach. With his brute strength and ability to run over opposing players, he won games for us. Some games he carried the ball on almost every play. He made victory possible, and that made the game somewhat enjoyable and practices on dusty fields bearable.

The thought of Don running over me still brings a smile to my face, even though I can't breathe as well as I should.

Questions for Discussion

1. The author believed he needed to play football as a "rite of passage" to become a man. What do you see as important in order to pass from a child to an adult?

2. Have you personally benefited by organized sports? Explain.

3. It was common in the days of Coach K to hold up Ray Jones as a role model player. Would you agree with Coach K? Explain.

4. Do you spend more time playing sports or watching sports on television? What happens when viewing exceeds playing time? Discuss.

When My Father Was a Boy

W hat was it like when you were a boy?" I once
asked my father. I knew my father was a boy
in the days before people sprayed graffiti on buildings
or killed others in drive-by shootings. So I didn't have
to ask him whether he went to school with taggers or
gangsters.

My father did not answer me directly. He took a
picture down from the wall of his study and showed
me a photo of his college gradation class. He was still
a teenager at the time of his graduation from college
in Genoa, Italy. There were twenty students in the
photo and as many professors.

"School was different when I was a boy. As you can
see in this picture, we had almost a one-to-one ratio
between teacher and student by the time we got to
the upper high school level. Many young people did
not get past the first few years of grade school.

"In those days it was all right to drop out of school.
If you had the desire to learn, you could advance
through grade levels very rapidly. Two of my brothers
did not like school very much. One went to work as a
day laborer and the other joined the army. When I
was a boy, no one was forced to attend school. But
you were expected to work. Life was different and
schools were different when I was a boy."

I told my father about an incident at my high
school during my freshman year. The Latin teacher

did not like the fact that a student was slouched in his seat with a toothpick in his mouth. In anger the teacher hit the student in the face with the force of his open hand. My father said such an incident would have been unlikely in his day.

My father went on: "By the time I was fourteen, I was preparing for my life work. I saw teachers punish children in the early grades. By the time a young man was thirteen or fourteen in the old country, he was expected to be a serious student. My education was very personal. By comparison with students in this country, few had the opportunity. I suppose I was one of the lucky ones."

Having earned his college degree by the age of nineteen, my father came to the United States of America to find work. When he arrived in Los Angeles, California, in 1923, the city was still like a village surrounded by farmland.

In those days immigrants were welcome in California because there was much work to do on the railroads, on the farms, in the factories, and in offices.

My father worked hard for many years as an accountant. Working hard came to him naturally. As he grew older, he became concerned because the city he loved, Los Angeles, had so many problems. Buildings that he once took pride in were disfigured with ugly graffiti. There were homeless people living on the sidewalks of a once proud downtown area that had provided work for the poor from other countries. He was dismayed by the reports of gang killings in neighborhoods he once knew as peaceful.

My father had come from a "big city," the ancient seaport of Genoa. Certainly Genoa must have had its share of crime with sailors coming home on leave and all the other components of city life. I asked my father if he had any memory of himself or any of his brothers getting into trouble with the law. He

searched his memory for an example and came up
with the following:

"In those days we were not conscious of police. I do
not ever remember any type of situation with a
policeman. The authority figure I remember best was
my parish priest. He was the man who had the most
control over our lives. I remember how mothers would
send their sons to the priest for confession if they
stole a loaf of bread or candy from the local store. The
priest would give the boy a sound scolding and some
work to do."

My father described the typical prank that a young
man might commit: telling an off-color joke or
sneaking into the inner sanctum of a church to steal a
drink of the wine used in services. The "juvenile
delinquent" as the term is used today was almost
nonexistent.

I asked, "Do you think the world of today is better
or worse than the world of your early years?"

It was a difficult question for my father. He had
left the "old world" for a better life in the "new world."
He was aware that there were no new opportunities
as had existed in the 1920s. He had sensed that his
generation had struggled to make the world a better
and safer place for children. He understood why there
were gangs because he came from a country where
organized crime (the Mafia) had intimidated poor
people for centuries. He was aware of the history of
Italy, where cities fought their own version of gang
wars for centuries. He knew about good and evil.
More than anything he was saddened that people
with wealth allowed America to disintegrate so
quickly.

The world that my father left when he died in 1994
was certainly more complicated than the world he
was born into in 1904. In the span of his lifetime he
saw all the progress that resulted from the
automobile, the airplane, nuclear weapons, and space

travel. But as a student of history, he knew that in a world where children were neglected the idea of using material progress to measure social progress was deceptive. This is why in his later years he supported a program to help young men who dropped out of school. My father did not understand the rapid deterioration of a society he had helped to build, but he was one of the "good guys" who did his part to make the world more peaceful.

Suggestions for Discussion

1. How do you think you would have completed high school if you grew up in the days of the author's father (early 1900s)?

2. What differences do you see in your educational opportunities by comparison with the opportunities given your parents?

3. Describe what you believe is the strongest quality of your father or the man who was most influential in your childhood?

4. If you were the "Education Tzar" for the United States, what would you do to help resolve some of our education problems?

The Little Soldier

When my mother was eighty-seven, disabled from illness and close to death, she surprised me by reciting a poem she had learned as a young girl. The poem, which was in the French language, was entitled "Le Petit Soldat" ("The Little Soldier"). The poem, as I understood my mother's French, went something like this:

> The little soldier marched off to the
>   battlefield,
> Leaving his mother, his friends, his work,
>   and his sweetheart.
> The smile on his lips could not hide the tears
>   in his eyes.
> With his gun he marched to the front
> To fight for justice, for honor, and for his
>   beloved land.

I asked my mother how she had come to learn this poem that had stayed in her memory for seventy-five years. She told me of the man who taught her the poem, her blind French teacher.

The year was 1918. My mother lived with her parents in Los Angeles, California. The First World War was still fresh in everyone's memory. Hollywood was producing movies. Women dancers, known as "flappers," were very popular. My grandparents, being protective of my mother, decided she should do

her high school years in the more conservative setting
of a village in Southern Italy. Thus, it came to pass
that my mother met the blind French teacher of
Southern Italy who inspired her to memorize "Le
Petit Soldat."

Everyone in the small town knew the life story of
the French teacher. As a young man he was inducted
into the army to fight in the First World War. All
wars are ugly. But the First World War was
considered by many historians the ugliest and
deadliest war ever imagined by the human race.
Hundreds of thousands of soldiers died in muddy
trenches, many from poison gas and untreated
wounds. Worst of all, no one knew why the war was
being fought. Soldiers simply put on a uniform, were
given a gun, and went out to die in trenches at the
hands of other soldiers who also did not know why
they were fighting.

It was in these circumstances that my mother's
French teacher became blind from a self-inflicted
wound. He was upset at being called into the army to
fight a war he neither believed in nor understood. His
government did not respect a person's right to refuse
to fight. He decided he would kill himself rather than
be forced to kill another person. So he shot himself.
He did not die. But his gunshot wound left him blind.

My mother was very fond of her French teacher in
the little Italian town. She enjoyed talking to him
about all the joys and sorrows of life.

The world in which my mother grew up did not
question much the reasons for war. Like the little
soldier in the poem, young men simply went to war
without any questioning. They were called
unpatriotic if they did not fight. They left their loved
ones at home and went to fight for the glory of some
"fatherland" or "motherland."

I wondered why, out of all the lessons my mother
learned, she remembered best a French poem about a

102

little soldier. French was not her native language. And she had never really known a soldier; nor had she known war.

Perhaps we never completely realize the things that affect us when we are young, the kind of things that stay in our memories. My mother was about twelve years old when she memorized "The Little Soldier" in its original French. Seventy-five years later she could recite it with the same enthusiasm as a schoolgirl. I believe my mother held this poem in her soul's memory because it had a certain universal sadness we all feel. A young soldier sent to war is usually portrayed as bold and patriotic, but often he is frightened and does not know his government's real reasons for war. I believe my mother also held this poem close to her heart because in truth it was about her French teacher, himself a strange victim of the war he did not want to fight.

Questions for Discussion

1. Why do you think the author's mother remembered this poem? Was there a connection between the poem and her teacher?

2. What are your feelings when you hear of young men being sent to war zones? Discuss.

3. Would you say the French teacher was a coward? Why or why not?

4. Debate: Should a young man or woman be forced to participate at some level in a war of his or her government?

More Resources for Working with Young People

STREET SMARTS:
Activities That Help Teenagers Take Care of Themselves

Dr. Michael Kirby

Paper, 128 pages, 8½" x 11", ISBN 0-89390-331-0

Teenagers start out in the relatively secure environment of home and school. Somehow they must learn how to make it in the more hazardous world of work and adulthood. They have to learn how to take care of themselves. This book examines the many roadblocks in their way and helps them explore how to overcome them. Case studies, role-plays, and activities involve them in the process and make the learning fun. A great resource for a variety of classrooms and small groups. Could be used as a course or as pick-and-choose activities. Includes permission to photocopy student handouts.

ACTING IT OUT JUNIOR:
Discussion Starters for 10 to 13 Year Olds

Marsh Cassady and Joan Sturkie

Paper, 160 pages, 6" x 9," ISBN 0-89390-240-3

Short dramatic sketches to help start discussions on issues of critical importance to junior high and middle school students: abuse, alcoholism in the family, dating, drug use, gang activity, homosexuality, cheating, shoplifting, and more.

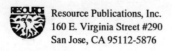